This is Anita's big day. She looks at her face in the mirror. "I can be a movie star, I *know* I can!" she thinks. She takes a letter out of her bag and reads it again. "Dear Miss Rosselli, Come to the movie studio at 10 o'clock on Tuesday morning. Mr Stein can see you then." She hears the telephone and answers it.

"Oh Dan. It's you," she says.

This is Dan's big day. He has a new car. It is fast, and red, and beautiful. "Anita likes men with fast cars," Dan thinks. "Now I can take her out."

He has a telephone in his car. He calls Anita's number. "Hi, Anita," Dan says. "Come out with me in my new car." "OK," Anita says. "You can take me to the movie studio." Dan drives to Anita's house.

"Anita!" Dan says. "I love your dress. And your hair! You look beautiful!" "Thanks, Dan," Anita says. "Let's go. Mr Stein wants to see me at 10 o'clock."

Dan drives very fast down the highway. "Wow! You're a good driver!" Anita says. Dan is happy. He is not looking at the road. He is looking at Anita. He does not see the STOP sign at the end of the highway.

"Where's the road? Where are we?" Dan says. There are a lot of trucks here, but he cannot see any cars. "Follow that big truck," Anita says.

He follows the truck. It turns right, but Dan drives on. "Where are we?" Anita says. "Hey," Dan says. "We've got a problem! Shut your eyes, Anita. Don't look." The car goes up and up. "Don't open your eyes," Dan says.

The car comes down and down. “You can open your eyes now,” Dan says. “Look, we’re on the road again.” He drives across the grass to the road. It is very big and very long. There is a line of lights beside it.

“Look at this,” Dan says. “Our car is the only car on the road. Let’s go really fast.” Anita laughs. “I love fast cars,” she says.

Suddenly Anita hears something behind her. "What's that?" she says. She is not laughing now. "Oh no! An airplane! Why is there an airplane on this road?" Dan does not answer. He is driving very fast. He stays in front of the airplane and it goes over his head. Anita is crying. "Dan, what are you doing?" she says. "Stop the car! I want to get out!"

Dan does not stop the car. "It's OK, Anita," he says. "We're all right. Don't forget, we're going to the movie studio. You want to be there at 10 o'clock."

Anita remembers Mr Stein. She looks at her watch. "You're right," she says. "I don't want to be late. Let's go fast again." Dan follows the EXIT signs out of the airport.

Long lines of cars are on the airport road. Dan cannot go fast now. "How far is the studio?" he asks Anita. "About a mile," she says. "This is a really bad road," says Dan. "Let's go down there."

Dan turns the car into a small road. He can go fast again now. But suddenly, the road stops. Dan does not stop. He drives under the trees and across the grass.

The car comes to a river. There is a bridge, but it is only for people on foot. Dan looks at the bridge and thinks. Then he says, “Watch this.”

Anita knows Dan now. “No!” she says. “Stop, Dan! Please! I can’t swim!” She wants to open the car door and jump out. But Dan is driving onto the bridge. Anita’s face is white. She cannot speak. She shuts her eyes.

Dan drives off the bridge and stops. “You see?” he says. “It’s easy, isn’t it?”

A very important person is watching Dan from the line of cars. But Dan does not see him. He starts the car again and drives up onto the road. Now they are in front of the traffic. “Look!” says Anita. “We’re almost at the studio. Oh Dan, you’re a fantastic driver!”

The car stops at the gate of the studio. "Who do you want to see?" the man asks. "Have you got a letter? You can't come in without a letter." "I've got a letter from Mr Stein," Anita says, "but it's at home."

Dan is angry. "Mr Stein wants to see her at 10 o'clock," he says. "Open the gate." "I can't," the man says. "I'm sorry."

Dan puts his foot down and turns the wheel. The car jumps. "Hey!" the man says. "You can't ..." The car is going very fast on two wheels. The gate is behind it now.

Anita gets out of the car at the door of the studio. "Go in, Anita," Dan says. "You're a star, I know you are. You can get the job." Anita goes up to the door.

A long, black car arrives at the studio door. A big man with a cigar gets out. "Are you from a circus, or something?" the man says. "You drive off the highway, under an airplane, across a footbridge, through the gate ... Who are you?" "My name's Dan," Dan says, "and I like driving cars. Who are *you?*" "I'm Mr Stein," the man says. "I'm the boss of this movie studio."

“Do you want a job, Dan?” Mr Stein says. “What job?” Dan asks. “I want a driver in my new movie,” Mr Stein says. “It’s a very difficult job. Can you drive off the roof of a building?” “Easy,” Dan says. “Can you drive into a river?” “Of course,” Dan says. “Good,” Mr Stein says. He looks at Anita. “Are you the Rosselli girl?” he says. “You’re short. I want a tall girl. I’m sorry.”

"Wait a minute," Dan says. "You want me, you take Miss Rosselli too." He gets into his car. "Stop! Don't go!" Mr Stein says. He looks at Anita again. "Can you dance?" he says. "Easy," Anita says. She dances. "Good," Mr Stein says. "Can you sing?" "Of course," Anita says. She sings. "OK, OK," Mr Stein says. "You win. Miss Rosselli, you start on Monday too."

Questions

1 When does Mr Stein want to see Anita? (*page 1*)

2 Why does Dan drive off the road? (*page 4*)

3 What flies over Dan's car? (*page 6*)

4 How do Dan and Anita cross the river? (*page 9*)

5 Who is watching Dan and Anita from the road? (*page 10*)

6 Why doesn't the man at the studio open the gate? (*page 11*)

7 Who is the man with the big cigar? (*page 13*)

8 What job does Mr Stein give Dan? (*page 14*)

9 When will Anita start work at the studio? (*page 15*)

Puzzle

1 Anita's last .... is Roselli.

2 Dan doesn't see the .... sign.

3 There's a bridge across the ....

4 .... wants to be a movie star.

5 Mr .... is the boss of the movie studio.

6 Dan likes .... cars.

7 Anita doesn't want to arrive .... at the studio.

8 .... is a very good driver.

9 Mr Stein has a big black ....

1					
2					
3					
4					
5					
6					
7					
8					
9					

Ideas

1 Draw or paint ....

- a map of Dan and Anita's journey from her house to the movie studio.
- the kind of car that you would like to drive.

2 Write the story of Mr Stein's new movie with big parts for Anita and Dan.